KILLER WHALES

THE WHALE DISCOVERY LIBRARY

Sarah Palmer

Illustrated by David Palmer

Rourke Enterprises, Inc.
Vero Beach, Florida 32964

Library of Congress Cataloging-in-Publication Data

Palmer, Sarah, 1955-
  Killer Whales.

  (The Whale discovery library)
  Includes index.
  Summary: Describes the physical characteristics,
habits, and natural environment of the Killer whale,
whose powerful teeth and jaws make it possible for it
to eat other animals.
  1. Killer Whales—Juvenile literature.   [1. Killer
Whale.   2. Whales] I. Title. II. Series:
Palmer, Sarah, 1955-
Whale discovery library.
QL737.C432   1989   599.5'3   88-3272
ISBN 0-86592-481-3

Printed in the USA

TABLE OF CONTENTS

Killer Whales   5
How They Look   6
Where They Live   9
What They Eat   11
Living In The Ocean   14
Baby Killer Whales   16
Killer Whales and People   19
Saving Killer Whales   20
Fact File   22
Glossary   23
Index   24

KILLER WHALES

Killer whales are **toothed whales**, which means that they have teeth to eat fish and meat. Not all whales have teeth. Killer whales have teeth that fit tightly together and are very strong. They are called killer whales because their powerful jaws and teeth allow them to eat other animals. Sometimes killer whales eat whales even larger than themselves.

ller whales have powerful jaws and teeth

HOW THEY LOOK

Killer whales are black with large white markings on their undersides and on the side of the head. Killer whales have the longest **dorsal fin** of any whale. The dorsal fin of the male can be as long as 6 feet. Killer whales are medium-sized whales. The male grows to an average of 30 feet long and the female is about 18 feet long. A male killer whale usually weighs around 9 tons.

Male killer whales have very lor dorsal fins

WHERE THEY LIVE

Killer whales live in the cold waters of the northern Pacific and Atlantic Oceans. They are often seen off the western coast of North America, near Alaska and British Columbia. Killer whales also live south of Africa and Australia in the cold **Antarctic** seas. In the winter, families of killer whales **migrate** to warmer waters. That's where the young are born.

ler whales like cold water

WHAT THEY EAT

Killer whales are fun to watch, but they can be very deadly. As few as five and sometimes as many as fifty killer whales hunt together in packs. They attack all kinds of fish. They also eat other animals, like seals and penguins, that are found in the icy regions where the whales live. If a killer whale sees a seal sitting on an **ice floe**, he may ram his body against it to make the seal fall off. He then eats the seal.

*ller whales sometimes eat
seals*

Killer whales are usually found groups

Iler whales have beautiful black
and white markings

LIVING IN THE OCEAN

All whales are **mammals**, and they need air to breathe. They cannot breathe underwater. Killer whales come to the surface of the water to breathe. They breathe through a hole in the top of their head, which is known as a **blowhole**. The whales keep their blowhole closed while they are underwater. They open it when they want to breathe in and out at the surface.

Killer whales breathe throug blowholes

BABY KILLER WHALES

At the end of the summer the killer whale family has completed the long **migration** from cold to warm waters. They may have journeyed from Alaska past the coast of California to Mexico. The killer whale **calves** are born while the family is in warm waters. At birth the baby whale has the same patterned markings as its parents. The patches are yellow, but they turn white as the calf grows up. The killer whale calf stays close to its mother for the first year of his life. It is very playful.

*Killer whale calves stay close
their mothers*

KILLER WHALES AND PEOPLE

Killer whales can be seen in many marine parks and zoos in the United States. These whales are members of the dolphin family and perform similar tricks. They leap right out of the water. Sometimes killer whales like to stand on their tails with their heads out of the water. Although killer whales are cruel to other animals in the ocean, they are very gentle and playful in the marine parks.

ler whales are fun to watch at the marine park

SAVING KILLER WHALES

No creatures in the ocean dare to threaten the fierce killer whales. Their only **predators** are man. Killer whales are hunted and captured for marine parks. They are popular because they learn different tricks very fast and are fun to watch. So many killer whales have been captured for zoos that for a while many people worried that none would be left in the ocean. Today you must have a permit to take killer whales from the ocean.

Many killer whales were caug
for zoos

FACT FILE

Common Name:	Killer Whale, Orca
Scientific Name:	Orcinus orca
Type:	Toothed whale
Color:	Black with white patches
Size:	up to 30 feet
Weight:	up to 10 tons
Number in World:	Scientists have not counted how many killer whales live in the oceans. They are thought to be plentiful.

Glossary

Antarctic (ant ARC tic) — the area around the South Pole

blowhole (BLOW HOLE) — a nostril located on top of a whale's head

calf (CALF) — a young whale

dorsal fin (DOR sal FIN) — a fin on a whale's back

ice floe (ICE FLOE) — a sheet of floating ice

mammals (MAM mals) — animals that suckle their young

to migrate (MI grate) — to move from one place to another, usually at the same time each year

migration (mi GRA tion) — the movement from one place to another, usually at the same time each year

predators (PRED a tors) — animals that hunt others for food

toothed whale (TOOTHED WHALE) — a whale that has teeth used for feeding

INDEX

blowholes	14
breathe	14
dorsal fin	6
marine parks	19, 20
migration	16
size	22
teeth	5
weight	22